The PRINTERS

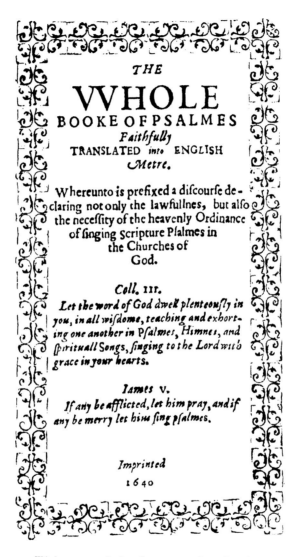

THE

VVHOLE

BOOKE OF PSALMES

Faithfully

TRANSLATED *into* ENGLISH

Metre.

Whereunto is prefixed a difcourfe de-
claring not only the lawfullnes, but alfo
the neceffity of the heavenly Ordinance
of finging Scripture Pfalmes in
the Churches of
God.

Coll. III.

*Let the word of God dwell plenteoufly in
you, in all wifdome, teaching and exhort-
ing one another in Pfalmes, Himnes, and
fpirituall Songs, finging to the Lord with
grace in your hearts.*

Iames V.

*If any be afflicted, let him pray, and if
any be merry let him fing pfalmes.*

Imprinted
1640

*Title page of the first complete book
published in the British American colonies*

COLONIAL CRAFTSMEN

The
PRINTERS

WRITTEN & ILLUSTRATED BY

Leonard Everett Fisher

BENCHMARK BOOKS

MARSHALL CAVENDISH
NEW YORK

For my children,
Julie, Susan, and James

Benchmark Books
Marshall Cavendish Corporation
99 White Plains Road
Tarrytown, NY 10591-9001

Copyright © 1965 by Leonard Everett Fisher

First Marshall Cavendish edition 2000

Library of Congress Cataloging-in-Publication Data
Fisher, Leonard Everett.
The printers / written and illustrated by Leonard Everett Fisher.
p. cm. — (Colonial craftsmen)
Includes index.
Summary: Surveys the history of printing in colonial America, describing
the work of the early printers, the development of the free press,
and the printer's craft and technique.
ISBN 0-7614-0929-7
1. Printing—United States—History—17th century—Juvenile literature.
2. Printing—United States—History—18th century—Juvenile literature. 3. Publishers
and publishing—United States—History—17th century—Juvenile literature.
4. Publishers and publishing—United States—History—18th century—Juvenile
literature. [1. Printing—History. 2. Printing.] I. Title. II. Series: Fisher, Leonard
Everett. Colonial craftsmen.
Z208.F5   1999   686.2'0973-dc21   99-33361   CIP

Printed and bound in the United States of America

1   3   5   6   4   2

A Short History

"E FIGHT NOT TO ENSLAVE, but to set a country free, and to make room upon the earth for honest men to live in."

This ringing cry for liberty was written by Thomas Paine during the American Revolution. It was printed on September 12, 1777, in a pamphlet called *The American Crisis*. The day before, General George Washington and his men had been defeated in a battle at Brandywine Creek, in Pennsylvania. Later that winter the ragged American army shivered on the frozen ground at Valley Forge.

Of all the colonial American craftsmen who used their skills to build a nation, none was as close to the spirit of liberty as was the printer. The words he printed on paper, whether they were his own or those of someone else, aroused the people with thoughts of freedom. And printed words sharpened the colonists' courage to fight on when their hopes of victory seemed dim. The printers' work in colonial America was as much a part of the fight for independence as were the

Valley Forge — the struggle for freedom

The Reverend Jose Glover
had printing equipment
loaded aboard ship

bloody battles that finally drove the British from the land.

But the story of the colonial printer did not begin with the War for Independence. It started in England in 1638, when America seemed a distant, lonely, and savage place, and when the Massachusetts Bay Colony was only eight years old. In that year the Reverend Jose Glover, a Puritan clergyman, decided to help bring civilization to America. He bought a printing press, some type and ink, a large amount of paper, and other equipment, and had them loaded aboard a ship called the *John.* Together with Stephen Daye, who was a locksmith hired to accompany him, and with their two families, Mr. Glover embarked for America. But he never arrived there. He died at sea.

Stephen Daye completed the journey, however. When the *John* reached America, Mrs. Glover put Stephen Daye in charge of the press and its printing. A house was provided for the Dayes in the tiny Puritan settlement of Cambridge, on the banks of the Charles River, just west of Boston. There Stephen Daye, with the

The *HISTORY*

help of his son Matthew, set up the first printing press in the British American colonies. Cambridge, the home of Harvard College, was a place of ideas, and a good location for a printing press.

But Stephen Daye could not print just anything he pleased. He operated his press by special permission granted by the government of the Massachusetts Bay Colony. And that colony was ruled, in turn, by England. If the government did not like what Daye printed it could take away his license. He would then be unable to go on printing.

The church authorities also had a great deal to say about what Stephen Daye could print. They provided much of the work for him. If the church pastors did not approve of what was being printed, they could simply stop sending work to the press. If that were to happen, Stephen Daye would lose business.

And so it happened that the first thing printed in British America on the Daye press was "The Free-man's Oath," a statement of allegiance which citizens must agree to. This was printed in 1639. Another of the early works of the press was for

the church. It was *The Whole Booke of Psalmes*, now often known as the "Bay Psalm Book." It appeared in 1640, and was the first full-length book published in the British colonies of America.

In 1649, Samuel Green became the printer at the press, and Stephen Daye went into another business. In 1660, Green started to print a work for the Reverend John Eliot, a missionary to the Indians. It was a translation of the English Bible into the language of the native Algonquins. Samuel Green was later helped by Marmaduke Johnson, and the work was finished in 1663.

Marmaduke Johnson was not content to work under the watchful eye of another person, however. In 1665 he bought a press and type of his own. Against the wishes of the church officials, he asked for government permission to set up a press in Boston. After some trouble, he received permission and went about establishing his press across the Charles River. Unfortunately, he died before he could start operating it. Nevertheless, by refusing to surrender his right to print what and where he pleased, Johnson supported the idea that in America the printers should be free to decide about their work for themselves.

The *HISTORY*

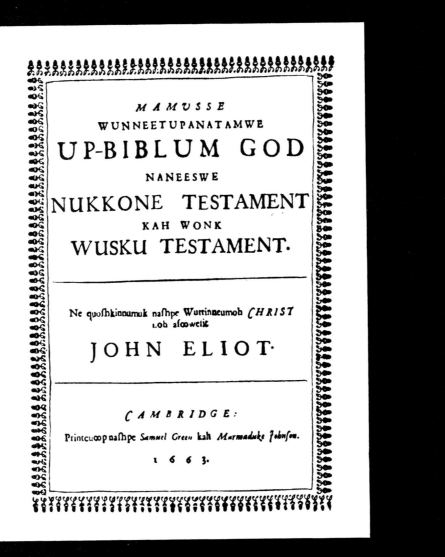

MAMUSSE

WUNNEETUPANATAMWE

UP-BIBLUM GOD

NANEESWE

NUKKONE TESTAMENT

KAH WONK

WUSKU TESTAMENT.

Ne quoſhkinnumuk naſhpe Wuttinneumoh *CHRIST*
ιoh aſœwelit

JOHN ELIOT·

CAMBRIDGE:

Printcuœop naſhpe *Samuel Green* kah *Marmaduke Johnſon.*

1 6 6 3.

Front page of the
New-York Gazette *for the week*
of November 28, 1726

Some years later, another printer dared to be critical of church authorities. He was William Bradford of Philadelphia, Pennsylvania.

Bradford had come to America with an early group of Quakers. In 1685, three years after his arrival on Pennsylvania soil, he started Philadelphia's first printing press.

The Quakers feared that printers were troublemakers. Yet Bradford was permitted to work for eight years. Then in 1693 he wrote and printed a series of pamphlets which some of the Quakers did not like. They brought him to a court trial, and forced him to move to New York. He went on with his work there, and in 1725 founded the city's first newspaper, the *New-York Gazette.*

The *New-York Gazette* was not British America's first newspaper. The very first one was *Publick Occurrences*, printed in Boston in 1690. It criticized the British in their war with the French, and so after one issue the paper was quickly stopped by the government. It had no license, anyway, so stopping it was an easy matter.

Nevertheless, the people of Boston were determined to have a better way of learning the latest

Numb. 57.

THE
New-York Gazette,

From *November* 28. to Monday *December* 5. 1726.

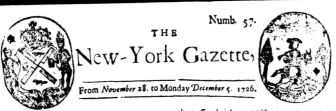

The SPEECH of the Honourable Patrick Gordon *Esq; Lieut. Governour of the Province of* Pennsylvania, *and Counties of* New-Castle, Kent & Sussex, *upon* Delaware.

To the Representatives of the Freemen of the said Province of *Pennsylvania*, November 22d. 1726.

Mr. Speaker, and Gentlemen of the House of Representatives;

HAVING fully declared to the last Assembly, what I take to be incumbent on me, in the Discharge of my Trust; I shall now recommend to you such Matters relating to the Publick, as may be proper for your Consideration.

And in the first Place our Bills of Credit will claim your Regard: At your first Meeting in *October*, I acquainted you with a Letter, I had received but two Days before, from the Secretary to the Right Honourable the Lords Commissioners for Trade and Plantations, on the Subject of our *Paper-Currency*, which I now lay before you. By this Letter you will observe what Impressions the Conduct of some of these *American* Colonies had made on that Board, to the Disadvantage of such Bills: Yet notwithstanding their Dislike to them in general, They have express'd so much Tenderness for the People of this Province, who have now that *Currency* in their Hands, that we may, I hope, justly conclude the former Acts for establishing it are happily out of Danger of a Repeal. But as the Act past last Year, for the re-emitting part of the same Bills out of the Loan-Office, may be thought to interfere with their Lordships Directions; it will require our serious Application, to find out proper Measures for securing this equally with the other Acts; which 'tis hoped may be successfully effected, when their Lordships are duly apprized, that the Trade between *Britain* and this Province has been so far from Suffering, that it has been manifestly encreased since the Establishment of that *Currency* here, and that more *British* Goods have been imported, more Ships Built in this Place for their Merchants, than had been for many Years before: But more especially that this *Currency* instead of sinking in Value, which has been the great and chief Objection to it in some other Colonies, now actually rises with us, being at this Time at less than half the Discount, that, as I have

been assured, it bore with Gold and Silver, but a few Months before my Arrival. When this is July represented to their Lordships, I hope we shall have no Room to doubt, but they will abate in their Opinions of the ill Consequences of that *Currency*, especially in this Colony: And therefore seeing *Ten Thousand Pounds* of the Bills now in the People's Hands, subsist on the Foundation of the last Act, which was past before their Lordships Sentiment were made known to us, we may hope for their Indulgence to that also. To obtain which I shall very heartily joyn with you Gentlemen, in whatever shall be reasonably proposed.

I cannot but with great Pleasure take Notice on this Occasion, of the happy Prospect that this Province now affords, of supplying, by the Industry of it's Inhabitants, the want of those natural Advantages, that have attended divers of the *American* Colonies (in making Returns with their own Product directly for *Britain*) which in all Probability must in due time introduce real Wealth, and a *Currency* of intrinsic Value amongst us. Several Companies are already engaged in carrying on *Iron Works*. *Hemp*, from the Incouragement given, I am told, is raised in much greater Quantities; But the first of these requiring a large Stock, and the other very fertile or enriched Land, which may disable poorer Families from partaking of their Benefits, Providence seems now to have pointed out one Method more, for Imploying even the mean and weak, as well as others of both Sexes, to considerable Advantage, by raising *Silk*; which (as I am credibly informed) is produced here, as fine and good, as most the World affords, and with as much Ease: These three are Commodities for which *Britain* pays dear to other Countries, and with which there can be no Danger of overstocking the Market: therefore as nothing can be more acceptable to *Britain*, than to receive from it's own Colonies, what it purchases more disadvantageously from Foreigners, nothing perhaps may better deserve the Notice and Encouragement of the Legislature.

These, *Gentlemen*, are the Heads I shall at present mention: What further occurs may be sent to you by Messages. I shall only here observe that from the Views I have yet had of this Province; it appears very plain, that we are, or may be, a very happy People; if we can but act worthy of those Blessings, which seem to have

attended

Front page of the
New-England Courant *for the week*
of February 4, 1723

happenings than by listening to the voice of the town crier or the town gossip. They wanted a newspaper. In 1704, John Campbell, the postmaster of Boston, started the *Boston News-Letter*.

The *HISTORY*

Fifteen years later, the *American Weekly Mercury* was founded in Philadelphia by Andrew Bradford, the son of William Bradford. In 1721, Boston had another newspaper, the *New-England Courant*. It was printed by James Franklin, older brother of Benjamin Franklin.

James Franklin began teaching the craft of printing to twelve-year-old Benjamin in 1718. By 1721, Benjamin was not only a skilled printer; he was also a talented writer. Unknown to his older brother, and using the name of "Mrs. Silence Dogood," fifteen-year-old Benjamin wrote various articles for the paper. The pieces were bright and sharp and original, and more people bought the paper because of them.

But Benjamin Franklin did not take kindly to being ordered about by his brother. In 1723, at the age of seventeen, he went to Philadelphia. There, in 1730, he purchased his own printing shop. From his press came *Poor Richard's Al-*

THE
New-England Courant.

From MONDAY February 4. to MONDAY February 11. 1723.

The late Publisher of this Paper, finding so many Inconveniencies would arise by his carrying the Manuscripts and publick News to be supervis'd by the Secretary, a. to render his carrying it on unprofitable, has intirely dropt the Undertaking. The present Publisher having receiv'd the following Piece, desires the Readers to accept of it as a Preface to what they may hereafter meet with in this Paper.

Non ego mordaci distrinxi Carmine quenquam,
Nulla venenato Litera mista Joco est.

LONG has the Press groaned in bringing forth an hateful, but numerous Brood of Party Pamphlets, malicious Scribbles, and Billingsgate Ribaldry. The Rancour and bitterness it has unhappily infused into Mens minds, and to what a Degree it has sowred and leaven'd the Tempers of Persons formerly esteemed some of the most sweet and affable, is too well known here, to need any further Proof or Representation of the Matter.

No generous and impartial Person then can blame the present Undertaking, which is designed purely for the Diversion and Merriment of the Reader. Pieces of Pleasancy and Mirth have a secret Charm in them to allay the Heats and Tumors of our Spirits, and to make a Man forget his restless Resentments. They have a strange Power to tune the harsh Disorders of the Soul, and reduce us to a serene and placid State of Mind.

The main Design of this Weekly Paper will be to entertain the Town with the most comical and diverting Incidents of Humane Life, which in so large a Place as Boston, will not fail of a universal Exemplification: Nor shall we be wanting to fill up these Papers with a grateful Interspersion of more serious Morals, which may be drawn from the most ludicrous and odd Parts of Life.

As for the Author, that is the next Question. But tho' we profess our selves ready to oblige the ingenious and courteous Reader with most Sorts of Intelligence, yet here we beg a Reserve. Nor will it be of any Manner of Advantage either to them or to the Writers, that their Names should be published; and therefore in this Matter we desire the Favour of you to suffer us to hold our Tongues: Which tho' at this Time of Day it may sound like a very uncommon Request, yet it proceeds from the very Hearts of your Humble Servants.

By this Time the Reader perceives that more than one are engaged in the present Undertaking. Yet is there one Person, an Inhabitant of this Town of Boston, whom we honour as a Doctor in the Chair, or a perpetual Dictator.

The Society had design'd to present the Publick with his Effigies, but that the Limner, to whom he was presented for a Draught of his Countenance, descryed (and this he is ready to offer upon Oath) Nineteen Features in his Face, more than ever he beheld in any Humane Visage before; which so rallied the Price of his Picture, that our Master himself forbid the Extravagance of coming up to it. And then besides, the Limner objected a Schism in his Face, which splits it from his Forehead to a strait Line down to his Chin, in such sort, that Mr. Painter protests it is a double Face, and he'll have Four Pounds for the Pourtraiture. However, tho' this double Face has spoilt us of a pretty Picture, yet we all rejoiced to see old Janus in our Company.

There is no Man in Boston better qualified than Janus for a Couranteer, or if you please, an Observator, being a Man of such remarkable Opticks, as to look two ways at once.

As for his Morals, he is a chearly Christian, as the Country Phrase expresses it. A Man of good Temper, courteous Deportment, found Judgment; a mortal Hater of Nonsense, Foppery, Formality, and endless Ceremony.

As for his Club, they aim at no greater Happiness or Honour, than the Publick be made to know, that it is the utmost of their Ambition to attend upon and do all imaginable good Offices to good Old Janus the Couranteer, who is and always will be the Readers humble Servant.

P. S. Gentle Readers, we design never to let a Paper pass without a Latin Motto if we can possibly pick one up, which carries a Charm in it to the Vulgar, and the learned admire the pleasure of Construing. We should have obliged the World with a Greek scrap or two, but the Printer has no Types, and therefore we intreat the candid Reader not to impute the defect to our Ignorance, for our Doctor can say all the Greek Letters by heart.

His Majesty's Speech to the Parliament, October 11. tho' already publish'd, may perhaps be new to many of our Country Readers; we shall therefore insert it in this Day's Paper.

His MAJESTY's most Gracious SPEECH to both Houses of Parliament, on Thursday October 11. 1722.

My Lords and Gentlemen,

I Am sorry to find my self obliged, at the Opening of this Parliament, to acquaint you, That a dangerous Conspiracy has been for some time formed, and is still carrying on against my Person and Government, in Favour of a Popish Pretender.

The Discoveries I have made here, the Informations I have received from my Ministers abroad, and the Intelligences I have had from the Powers in Alliance with me, and indeed from most parts of Europe, have given me most ample and current Proofs of this wicked Design.

The Conspirators have, by their Emissaries, made the strongest Instances for Assistance from Foreign Powers, but were disappointed in their Expectations: However, confiding in their Numbers, and not discouraged by their former ill Success, they resolved once more, upon their own Strength, to attempt the subversion of my Government.

To this End they provided considerable Sums of Money, engaged great Numbers of Officers from abroad, secured large Quantities of Arms and Ammunition, and thought themselves in such Readiness, that had not the Conspiracy been timely discovered, we should, without doubt, before now have seen the whole Nation, and particularly the City of London, involved in Blood and Confusion.

The Care I have taken has, by the Blessing of God, hitherto prevented the Execution of their traiterous Projects. The Troops have been incamped all this Summer; six Regiments (though very necessary for the Security of that Kingdom) have been brought over from Ireland; The States General have given me assurances that they would keep a considerable Body of Forces in readiness to put such on their first No-

Front page of the
Pennsylvania Gazette *for the week*
of October 22, 1730

manack, and a newspaper, the *Pennsylvania Gazette.* And from his shop came a famous patriot, diplomat, scientist, inventor, author, and thinker — one of America's great men, who wrote of himself as "I, Benjamin Franklin, Printer. . . ."

The *HISTORY*

Perhaps Benjamin Franklin, in wanting to be known first and foremost as a printer, was anxious for people to know of his humble beginnings. Perhaps, in calling attention to the fact that he was a printer, Benjamin Franklin was voicing his belief in the power of the printed word to move men's minds to do good or evil. Whatever the reason, he certainly knew that one of the first battles for freedom waged between Britain and America centered around a printer and his press. The printer was John Peter Zenger, editor of the *New-York Weekly Journal.*

Zenger was arrested by the British in 1735 for printing articles that criticized the colonial governor. The law was clear in this matter, and Zenger had broken it. Andrew Hamilton, the lawyer who defended Zenger, argued at the trial, however, that Zenger had merely printed the truth. He said that the jury should be allowed to con-

Numb. CII.

THE

Pennſylvania *GAZETTE*.

Containing the freſheſt Advices Foreign and Domeſtick.

From Thurſday, October 22. to Thurſday, October 29. 1730.

The SPEECH of the HONOURABLE

Patrick Gordon, Eſq;

Lieutenant Governor of the Counties of *New-Caſtle*, *Kent* and *Suſſex* on *Delaware*, and Province of *Pennſylvania*.

To the Repreſentatives *of the ſaid Counties in* General Aſſembly *met, at* New-Caſtle, *the* 21ſt *of* October, 1730.

GENTLEMEN,

MY ſteady Endeavours to put in Practice as well his late ſacred Majeſty's Commands to Me, which I mentioned at My firſt Arrival here, as My Inſtructions from our Honourable Proprietors, together with the happy Concurrence of the People in joining with what they manifeſtly ſaw was aimed ſolely at their own Good, have by Divine Providence been bleſſed with ſuch Succeſs, that now on Our annual Meeting, there ſeems little more Incumbent on Me, than to expreſs My Satisfaction in the Opportunity given Me of ſeeing the Repreſentatives of His Majeſty's good Subjects under my Care, convened together; and I hope it proves no leſs agreeable to You, GENTLEMEN, to have the ſame on Your Parts of meeting Me; that We may between Us ſhew that mutual Harmony, which will ever be the happy Reſult of a Diſpoſition in thoſe concerned in the Affairs of Our Government, to diſcharge their reſpective Duties with Loyalty to His Majeſty, Fidelity to Our Proprietors, and with Benevolence and Affection in every Individual towards his Neighbour.

The Continuance of this, GENTLEMEN, I heartily recommend to You, and that if Particulars ſhould yet harbour any Miſunderſtandings or private Uneaſineſſes, they ſhould, from a View of the Lovelineſs of Peace and publick Tranquility, entirely lay them aſide, that We may truly appear to all, what I think We really are, as happy a People among Ourſelves, as any in His Majeſty's Dominions.

GENTLEMEN,

You will now undoubtedly of Courſe, at this Meeting, take into Conſideration what yet remains from former Aſſemblies to be compleated or regulated; and herein, I hope, You will ſhew ſuch Unanimity, and make ſuch Diſpatch, as will fully prove We are all ſenſible of the Bleſſings we enjoy; and on My Part, nothing ſhall be wanting to improve them.

P. GORDON.

To the HONOURABLE

Patrick Gordon, Eſq;

Lieutenant Governor of the Counties of *New-Caſtle*, *Kent* and *Suſſex* on *Delaware*, and Province of *Pennſylvania*.

The Humble ADDRESS *of the* Repreſentatives *of the Freemen of the ſaid Counties, in* General Aſſembly *met, at* New-Caſtle *the* 22d *of* October, 1730.

May it pleaſe Your HONOUR,

WE, the Repreſentatives of theſe Counties, do with the greateſt Senſe of Gratitude, return Our ſincere Thanks for Your favourable and kind Speech to Us; and We are extreamly pleaſed that there appears to Your Honour ſo happy a Diſpoſition amongſt the People whom We repreſent, of Peace and Harmony, as that you do not find it neceſſary upon this Occaſion to to do more than expreſs Your Satisfaction in meeting Us at this Time; which next to the Divine Providence ariſes from the happy Effects of Your Honour's mild and prudent Adminiſtration; and we ſhould be wanting to Ourſelves, as well as Our Conſtituents, ſhould We, on Our Parts loſe any Opportunity of improving or maintaining the ſame: We ſhall at all Times endeavour to diſcharge Ourſelves with Duty and Loyalty to His Majeſty, Affection and all due Reſpect to Your Honour, and Fidelity to Our Proprietor.

It is a Bleſſing greatly to be valued, that there are not any Diſcontents or Miſunderſtandings
remaining

Front page of the
New-York Weekly Journal *for the*
week of April 7, 1735

sider not just whether Zenger had broken the law, but whether truth or falsehood had been printed. This was against the judge's wishes, but the jury agreed, and Zenger was set free.

Zenger's trial resulted in a famous victory for the idea that a printer should be free to print the facts, however unpleasant they might be to some people. From that day on and for the next forty years, England had to suffer the attacks on her authority made by furious colonists and their printing presses — printing what they felt to be the truth.

The *HISTORY*

Numb. LXXIV

THE
New - York Weekly JOURNAL

Containing the freſheſt Advices, Foreign, and Domeſtick.

MUNDAY April 7th, 1735.

Sir.

IN my former I ſhewed, that allowing all that Mr. *Murray* wanted to prove, *viz.* That the Jurifdiction of the great Courts of *England* extend to *New-York*, the preſent ſupream Court of *New-York*, cannot exiſt lawfully, and exercife the ſame Powers which thofe Courts have ; and I now further add, that no Ordinance of the Governor & Council, or even Act of the Legiſlature of this Province can give it the ſame Powers ; becauſe that cannot be done without deſtroying the Powers of the great Court of *England*, ſo far at leaſt as relates to this Province : For, *as* I obſerved, both cannot have the ſame Powers at the ſame Time and in the ſame Place, and the Legiſlature of this province has no Kind of Authority over the great Courts or any Courts in *England*.

Mr. *Murray* in ſome Part of his Opinion, ſays, that the Argument which proves too much proves nothing. And I ſay, when a Conclufion evidently falſe is drawn, it ſhews one or more of the Propofitions from whence it is deduced are falſe, and that the Arguer has made a Slip in the Deduction : For from Truth Truth always follows, and Truth never brings forth Falſhood. For this Reaſon its to examine Mr. *Murray*'s Propofitions.

The Firſt is, that the Great Courts in *England* are Fundamental Courts,

and this muſt be with Refpect to the Conſtitution : For if it be taken in any other Senſe, the Conclufion which he draws from it will not follow. The Word Fundamental comes from Foundation ; ſo that when we ſay any Thing is Fundamental of another we ſay, that that Thing is the Foundation where onthe other is built, and if we conceive that the Thing which is the Foundation be taken away we imediately perceive that the other Thing which is built upon it muſt tumble down, and fall to Pieces. Now I prefume that any Man may eaſily conceive how any one or all of the Courts in *England* may be diſſolved, and other Courts Eſtabliſhed in their Room, without the leaſt Injury to the Conſtitution ; and therefore I conclude, that thefe Courts are not Fundamental to the Conſtitution, as Mr. *Murray* ſuppofes, but that his firſt fundamental Propofition is falſe, and therefoe that all his Arguments built upon it muſt fall to the Ground- Its ſo eafie to conceive, how thefe Courts may be diſſolved, without injury to the Conſtitution, and others eſtabliſhed, that Mr. *Murray* would think me idle if I would take up Time to ſhew it. But to put it beyond Contradiction, and any Gentleman's Skill in Sophiſtry to perfwade any Man of Senſe, that the great Courts are Fundamental, that is ſuch without which our Conſtitution can't exiſt, we need only obſerve, that there are many Places in *England* which

How the Printers Worked

A PRINTER'S TOOLS

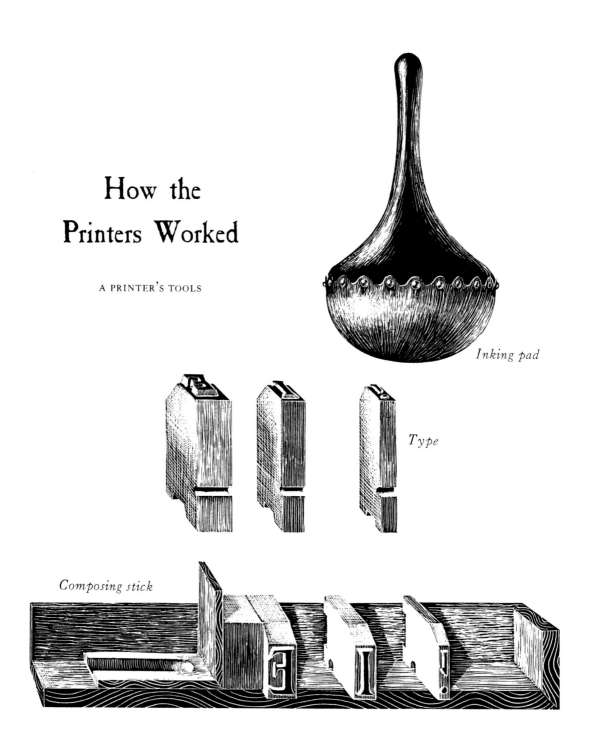

Inking pad

Type

Composing stick

PRINTING IS A MEANS OF PRESSING letters, words, sentences, and pictures onto a sheet of paper.

In order to do his work, the printer must have certain equipment. Chief among it are three things: metal type, ink, and a printing press.

The colonial printer's *type* was made up of a great number of single metal letters of the alphabet. They could be put together to make words and sentences, which could then be combined into pages. Once each page of type was inked, it could be printed in as many copies as were needed. Then the single metal letters could be separated. They could be used again and again, to make many different words and sentences and pages. They were called *movable* type, because the single letters could be moved about to make a variety of words.

John Gutenberg seems to have been the first man to work out practical ways of making type and putting it together with ink and a press to do a satisfactory job of printing. He did his work in Germany between the 1440's and the 1460's —

Compositor   *Making up a form*

Cleaning a form   *Printing*   *A colonial printing shop*

The *TECHNIQUE*

about two hundred years before Stephen Daye printed *The Whole Booke of Psalmes.*

A complete collection of all the type characters in the same size and style was called a *font.* It contained greater quantities of some letters than of others, because the printer would use more of them. He would use more E's than X's, for example. A printer bought as many type fonts as he might need or could afford.

Each piece of type had to be made in a special metal-working shop called a *type foundry.* There were no type foundries in British America in the early days. Nearly every piece of type used by the colonial American printers had to be imported from across the sea.

The early American printer was a man of many talents. He was a *writer.* He printed not only the written works of other people, but his own work as well. He was also an *editor,* a person who prepared and corrected the work at hand. He was a *publisher,* a person who issued printed material for sale. He was a *compositor,* a man who arranged the type letters into words, the words into sentences, and the sentences into

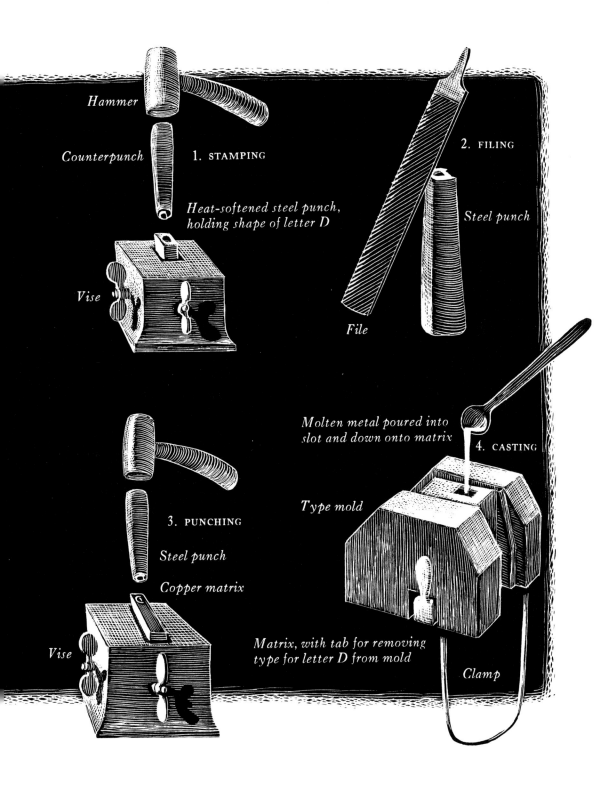

Hammer

Counterpunch

1. STAMPING

Heat-softened steel punch, holding shape of letter D

Vise

2. FILING

Steel punch

File

Molten metal poured into slot and down onto matrix

4. CASTING

Type mold

3. PUNCHING

Steel punch

Copper matrix

Matrix, with tab for removing type for letter D from mold

Vise

Clamp

pages. And he was a *pressman*, a person who operated a press.

If his printing shop was a large one, the printer employed skilled helpers to do some of these jobs. And he hired young *apprentices*, called *devils*, to work while at the same time they learned the printing craft. But if his shop was a small one, the printer did most of the work himself.

However large or small the shop might be, after the type arrived the next job belonged to the compositor. He placed the single pieces of type in a specially built shallow tray called a *case*. It was only an inch deep and was divided into two main sections. The upper section contained all the capital letters. Each kind of letter was put into a smaller section of its own, within the upper case — the K's in one little section, the W's in another, and so on. Thus, because of their location in the case, capital letters are still sometimes known as *upper case* letters.

The small letters were placed in their individual sections in the lower case. Hence these small letters are still known as *lower case* letters.

The letters were not arranged alphabetically,

The *TECHNIQUE*

A	B	C	D	E	F	G
H	I	K	L	M	N	O
P	Q	R	S	T	V	X
â	ê	î	ô	û	Y	Z
á		í	ó	ú	;	ſb
à	è	ì	ò	ù	ſk	ſl
*	ꝯ	J	U	j	ſt	ſſ

A	B	C	D	E	F	G
H	I	K	L	M	N	O
P	Q	R	S	T	V	X
J	U	Æ	æ	§	Y	Z
ffi	ë	Œ	œ	†	[ ]	!
fl	ï	ü	W	w	( )	?
ff	ﬅ	Ç	ç	É	é	"

°	ç	é	- ,	
&	b	c	d	e
z				
y	1	m	n	i
x	v	u	t	ſpaces

1	2	3	4	5	6	7	8
s		f	f	g	h	9	0
						æ	œ
				ffi	ffl	k	en quads
o		p	q	fi	fl	:	quads
a		r	.	,			em quads

but for convenience. The characters that would be used the most were placed nearest at hand. A beginning compositor's first job was to "learn the case" — learn the location of the letters so that he could reach for them without even looking.

The *TECHNIQUE*

When the compositor was ready to arrange, or *set*, the letters into words, he tacked the handwritten sheet of paper that he was to follow onto a reading stand fastened to the case. This handwritten sheet was called *copy*. Standing before the tilted type case and without taking his eyes off the copy, the compositor chose the proper letters and slid them one by one into a small, flat frame called a *composing stick*, which he held in his other hand.

When he had finished placing a single line in the stick, he spaced the letters and words out with slivers of brass so that the line would reach an exact measured length. Then he went on to the next line of type. When the composing stick was filled with lines all the same length, he removed them to a metal pan called a *galley*.

When the compositor had filled the galley with enough type to make one printed page, it was

Tapping the type in the form.
The man in background
holds a made-up form of type

inked and a rough print or *proof* was made of it. This *galley proof* was used to make any corrections or changes before the final printing.

The *TECHNIQUE*

After all the pages to be printed had been corrected, the set type was transferred from the galleys to a large, perfectly flat and smooth slab of *stone*. There the type was put into a large metal frame, or *chase*, and was locked in place so tightly that it could not fall out. Sometimes the printer locked up one page, sometimes two pages, but rarely more than four pages. It all depended on the job being done, and the size of the press. The pages locked into the chase were called the *form*.

Next, the printer lightly tapped the form with a flat piece of wood, to make the surface of the letters as level as possible. When this had been done, the form was ready for the press.

The early printing presses were wooden machines that stood a foot or two taller than a man. Running through the upright supports was a waist-high, table-like frame called a *carriage*. On the carriage was a wooden plank that slid back and forth along two rails. Fastened on top of the plank was another frame called a *coffin*.

Hinged to the coffin was the *tympan*, two tightly fitted frames over which was stretched parchment, much like that on a drum. The tympan held a soft padding useful in keeping the type from breaking under pressure when the paper was finally pressed against it. Another light frame was hinged to the tympan. It was called a *frisket.*

The printer placed the form in the coffin of the press. There, by means of two leather balls, he carefully inked the type. He then placed a sheet of paper on the tympan and folded the frisket over it, to hold it in place. The paper had been dampened in order to make sure that when it was pressed against the type it would lie flat and every inked piece of type would touch it.

The frisket and the tympan were again folded over. Now the paper that they held rested above the inked form in the coffin. The coffin was then slid along the carriage rails until it was directly under a four-inch-thick piece of hardwood called the *platen.*

The platen was attached to the bottom of a large *screw*, which in turn hung from a crossbar called the *head.* About halfway between the

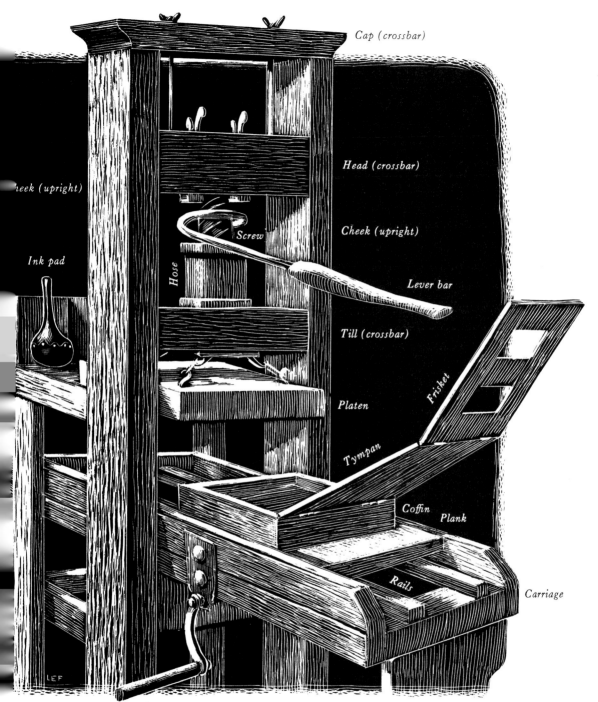

Cap (crossbar)

Head (crossbar)

Cheek (upright)

Screw

Lever bar

Hose

Till (crossbar)

Cheek (upright)

Ink pad

Frisket

Platen

Tympan

Coffin

Plank

Rails

Carriage

LEF

Spit handle (turns spit that rolls coffin under platen)

head and the platen was another crossbar called the *till.* The screw, enclosed in a box called a *hose,* passed through the till.

The *TECHNIQUE*

When all was ready, the printer put a bar into the screw and worked it down so that it pressed the platen onto the coffin. This pressure held the paper against the inked type. When the type letters had been printed on the paper, the platen was raised. Then the coffin, with the form, was rolled back to the end of the carriage. Here the frisket and the tympan were folded back, and the printed page was removed to a place where it could dry.

This process was repeated until the printer had as many copies or *impressions* of the page as were needed. Then the form was removed from the coffin and was washed with a solution of *alkali.* This alkali cut through the ink's thick substance and left the type clean. All the type pieces that made up the form were then returned to their proper places in the type case, to be used again later.

The colonial printer's method of printing a page was called *letterpress.* That is to say, it was a method by which a flat sheet of paper was pressed

Front page of the
Boston News-Letter *for the week*
of May 15, 1704

against a surface of raised letters that had been inked. This method, much modernized, is still used today in some forms of printing, and is still called *letterpress*.

The **TECHNIQUE**

The sturdy wooden presses used by the colonial printers were *sheet-fed, flat-bed* presses. That is, the printers placed paper, a sheet at a time, on a press which held the type in a flat, horizontal frame, or *bed*.

Some of these early printing presses were so strongly built that they were in continuous use for more than one hundred years. It should be remembered, however, that the presses used by the colonial printers were all made in Europe. It was not until some years after the Revolutionary War that Americans began to make their own presses.

Importing most of their tools and materials was bothersome to the colonial printers, but they made the best of it. Their real concern was for their product. And their product was printed words. They made sure that the paper, type, ink, and presses they used were the best they could get, so that the words and ideas they printed could be clearly and easily read by the people.

The Boston News-Letter.

Publifhed by Authority.

From Monday May 15. to Monday May 22. 1704.

Westminster, Novemb. 12. 1703.
The Addrefs of the Lords Spiritual and Temporal, prefented Her Majefty.

WEE Your Majefties moft dutiful and loyal Subjects, the Lords Spiritual and Temporal in Parliament Affembled, do offer up our hearty acknowledgments to Almighty God, for the prefervation of Your Royal Perfon, fo effential to the happinefs of Your People, & the Safety of *Europe.*

We fee, with the greateft fatisfaction, the zeal with which Your Majefty efpoufes the Publick Intereft, which carries You even beyond the obligations of Your Treaties in Defence of the Houfe of *Auftria,* againft the Ufurpations of the Houfe of *Bourbon,* & the glorious refituion of that Family to the Monarchy of *Spain,* which we have great reafon to expect from the late Alliance with the King of *Portugal,* will be chiefly owing to Your Majefties Arms and Affiftance.

Your Majefty may depend upon Security at home in the love of Your People, our Perfons & Fortunes fhall ever be ready to defend You upon all occafions, and Your Majefty may therefore, with the greater Safety and Glory, fend Your Fleets and Armies abroad in the Defence of Your Allies.

The happy Declaration of the Duke of *Savoy,* for the common Intereft, gives Your Majefty a feafonable opportunity to fhew Your Compaffion and concern for thofe Proteftants in the South of *France,* who lie under the heavieft Perfecution and oppreffion.

We lament for our felves and others the unavoidable expences of War, but have reafon to thank God and Your Majefty, that we are free from all the other Calamities of it, having almoft nothing elfe to wifh for (being fecured of a Proteftant Succeffion) but Your long and happy Reign over us: And we fhall moft willingly pay our proportion , encouraged by Your Royal Generofity for   ufe of Your People, & by the frugal management of what is given; being fenfible, there is no better way to fave the Wealth of the Nation, than by carrying on the War at this time with the utmoft vigour.

Your Majefty may expect from us a moft ready compliance with all Your defires, fo juftly merited by Your care of the general welfare and happinefs of Your People, extended even to the pooreft and meaneft of Your Subjects

This appears yet more eminently in that earneft and preffing Recommendation to Your Parliament of Union and Peace amongft themfelves; And we, in the moft folemn manner, Affure Your Majefty, That we will not only avoid, but oppofe whatfoever may tend to create any difquiet or difunion amongft Your Subjects.

We fhall never be wanting in any part of our Duty towards the Supporting Your Majefties honour & Your Allies, not doubting but Almighty God will profper Your Majefties Arms, fo glorioufly employed to protect all thofe whom the ambition of the *French* King would opprefs.

To which Her Majefty return'd Her moft Gracious Anfwer in thefe words.

My Lords,

I *Am extreamly fenfible of the particular concern You exprefs for me in this Addrefs, and of Your great zeal for the common caufe of Europe.*

I rely very much upon the Affurances You give me of Your Duty and Affection, and fhall always ufe my beft endeavours to eftablifh the fafety and happinefs of the Kingdom.

Pifcataqua, May, 13. Letters thence acquaint us of fome more damage, done by the Sculking Adverfary, on the 11. inftant *Nicholas Cole* of *Wells,* with *Nicholas Hogden, Thomas Dane* and *Benjamin Gough,* Souldiers, went about a Mile from Capt. *Wheelwright's* Garrifon to Look after his Cattle, and on their return were Attack't by 12. Indians, who kill'd faid *Cole* and *Hogden,* took *Dane* Captive, *Gough* efcaping, advifed Capt. *Hales* of it, who immediately called his Souldiers together; but the Enemy were fled.

Her Majefties Council by His Excy. direction hath appointed Thurfday the 18. inftant a day of Publick Fafting with Prayer, being the fame day appointed by His Excy. & Council in the Province of *Maff.Bay* and for faid ends contain'd in faid Proclamation.

Arrived here *John Holicom* from *Antigua, Richard Shortridge* for *Fyall* wind-bound. Outward-bound, Capt. *Alcock* for *Barbadoes* ready to Sail, *John Froft* for faid Port in Ten days, and *Robert Emery* in about 3 weeks, and *Richard Waterhoufe* for St. Chriftophers in a Week.

Northampton, May 13. A Company of Indians and French, between day break and Sun-rifing, about 60 Set upon a Garrifon-houfe of *Benj. Janes's,* about two Miles from the body of the Town, and fet fire to it ere they were aware of it ; Kill'd and carryed Captive about 30. Perfons. The Town being Alarmed, purfued them, the Enemy finding it, fcattered themfelves into parties ; and fo did the Englifh into Ten in a Company, purfuing them ; Capt. *Taylor* was kill'd in the purfuit.

Lisbon, March 27. On the advice brought the King of *Portugal,* of the Fleet from *England,* being on the Coaft in whom was the King of *Spain* ; he ordered a Wharff to be made from his Palace to the Waterfide, & overlaid it with Cloath of Scarlet, and went in his Barge on board to receive him, returned and the King of *Spain* on his right hand ; who was received with all imaginable Demonftrations of joy, by difcharing of Guns, ringing of Bells, bon-fires, illuminations, Fireworks, &c. and for a Fortnight nothing but Feafting. Three days ere the K. of *Spain* Arrived the Princefs (Daughter of the K. of *Portugal*) defigned to be his Queen, Dyed ; and that lofs like to made up by her Sifter, fome two years younger. Seven Grandees of *Spain* (befides thofe he brought with him) came to him upon his Arrival, who informed him that all places would fubmit to him affoon as he appeared. The Englifh and Dutch Forces were about 12 thoufand. The King of *Portugal* had 15. thoufand, and daily leavying of New Forces : Upon his Arrival he fent the Forces to the Fronteers, ; referving a few Companies for guard of his own Perfon to the Army, whither he defigned to March that Week, that Capt. *Elfon* came away & then directly for *Marid.* Upon the Fleets Arrival in *Lisbon,* confifting of about 22 Sail of Men of War, and about 300 Tranfport Ships : A Dutch Privateer being chafed by 5 Sail of Men of War, informed Admiral *Rook* of it,

Printers' Terms

CARRIAGE — The part of the printing press that held a movable plank, on top of which was fastened the coffin.

CASE — The shallow partitioned boxes that held the printer's type.

CHASE — The large metal frame into which type was locked into pages for printing.

COFFIN — Located on the carriage, this was the part of the press that held the form of type.

COMPOSING STICK — The hand frame in which the type was set into words and sentences.

FLAT-BED PRESS — A press that held the type on a flat, horizontal frame, or bed.

FONT — A complete collection of metal type characters in one size and style.

FORM — The locked-up type in the chase, to be printed into pages.

FRISKET — A light frame hinged to the tympan.

GALLEY — The metal tray into which the set type was transferred when the composer's stick was full.

HEAD — The crossbar on the press from which the screw was hung.

HOSE — The box which enclosed the screw as it passed through the till.

IMPRESSION — The inked likeness of the type on the paper.

LETTERPRESS — The method of printing by pressing a sheet of paper against inked type.

LOWER CASE — The lower part of the type case, which held the small letters; hence, the term "lower case" for small letters.

MOVABLE TYPE — Single metal letters that could be combined and recombined into any words wanted by the printer.

PLATEN — A four-inch-thick piece of hardwood attached to the bottom of the screw on the printing press.

PROOF — The inked impression of the type in the galley. From this, corrections were made.

SCREW — The part of the press that lowered the platen which applied pressure to the paper and inked form, and so made the final printed impression.

SET — To put type into a composing stick, to form words and sentences.

SHEET-FED PRESS — A press on which sheets of paper were fed, one at a time, to be printed.

STONE — The large, flat surface — formerly made of stone — on which the forms were made up.

TILL — The crossbar on the press, through which the screw passed.

TYPE — The single metal letters of the alphabet which the compositor combined into words for printing.

TYPE FOUNDRY — The shop where metal type was made.

TYMPAN — The tightly fitted frame over which parchment was stretched. The tympan was hinged to the coffin.

UPPER CASE — The upper part of the type case, in which the capital letters were kept; hence, the term "upper case" for capital letters.

Some Colonial American Printers

ADAMS, JAMES	*Wilmington, Delaware*	*(1761)**
BRADFORD, WILLIAM	*Philadelphia, Pennsylvania*	*(1685)*
	New York, New York	*(1693)*
DAVIS, JAMES	*Newbern, North Carolina*	*(1749)*
DAYE, STEPHEN	*Cambridge, Massachusetts*	*(1639)*
FOSTER, JOHN	*Boston, Massachusetts*	*(1675)*
FOWLE, DANIEL	*Portsmouth, New Hampshire*	*(1756)*
FRANKLIN, BENJAMIN	*Philadelphia, Pennsylvania*	*(1730)*
GREEN, SAMUEL	*Cambridge, Massachusetts*	*(1649)*
HASSELBACH, NICHOLAS	*Baltimore, Maryland*	*(1765)*
JOHNSON, MARMADUKE	*Cambridge, Massachusetts*	*(1665)*
	Boston, Massachusetts	*(1674)*
JOHNSTON, JAMES	*Savannah, Georgia*	*(1762)*
NUTHEAD, WILLIAM	*St. Mary's City, Maryland*	*(1685)*
PARKER, JAMES	*Woodbridge, New Jersey*	*(1754)*
PARKS, WILLIAM	*Williamsburg, Virginia*	*(1730)*
PHILLIPS, ELEAZER	*Charleston, South Carolina*	*(1731)*
RIND, WILLIAM	*Williamsburg, Virginia*	*(1766)*
SHORT, THOMAS	*New London, Connecticut*	*(1709)*
TIMOTHY, LEWIS	*Charleston, South Carolina*	*(1733)*

* *The date refers to the year in which these printers opened their shops*

Index

LEONARD EVERETT FISHER is a well-known author-artist whose books include *Alphabet Art, The Great Wall of China, The Tower of London, Marie Curie, Jason and the Golden Fleece, The Olympians, The ABC Exhibit, Sailboat Lost,* and many others.

Often honored for his contribution to children's literature, Mr. Fisher was the recipient of the 1989 Nonfiction Award presented by the *Washington Post* and the Children's Book Guild of Washington for the body of an author's work. In 1991, he received both the Catholic Library Association's Regina Medal and the University of Minnesota's Kerlan Award for the entire body of his work. Leonard Everett Fisher lives in Westport, Connecticut.